How to Develop Performance Instructional Activities and Evaluations

HOW TO WRITE AND USE PERFORMANCE OBJECTIVES TO INDIVIDUALIZE INSTRUCTION

Volume Four

How to Develop Performance Instructional Activities and Evaluations

Robert E. Boston

Educational Technology Publications
Englewood Cliffs, New Jersey 07632

This booklet is one of four parts of *How to Write and Use Performance Objectives to Individualize Instruction.*

Printed in the United States of America.

International Standard Book Number: 0-87778-040-4.

First Printing.

TABLE OF CONTENTS

As an educator, your task, in addition to writing performance objectives, is to construct evaluations and complete instructional programs with suggested methods and materials that will become the means by which the learner develops the skills and knowledge described by the performance objective. The design objective for this instructional program is related explicitly to these tasks and is stated as follows:

Given the directive to construct a terminal performance objective with related interim performance objectives and course objective* and a directive to write a test item and an instructional program to include suggested methods and materials to be used by the teacher in the instructional program, all directly relating to the test item, the educator will:

(a) Write a terminal performance objective with related interim performance objectives and course objectives,

(b) Construct a sample evaluation which reflects all of the interim performance objectives encompassed by the activity or course objective,

(c) Construct a self-directed activity that reflects one or more interim performance objectives,

(d) Describe methods and materials to be used by the teacher for three levels of instruction in each of the interim performance objectives included in the course objective but not included in the activity,

with 100 percent accuracy.

*A course objective is a translation of interim performance objectives in terms of specific skills or knowledge. Activity at the elementary level is equivalent to course objectives at the secondary level. (See Pages 56-60 in Volume 3 for complete explanation.)

This booklet is designed to aid you in developing the evaluations and an instructional program for the learner based on the following design: (To read flow chart, follow the arrows.)

INSTRUCTIONAL PROGRAM FOR A PERFORMANCE OBJECTIVE

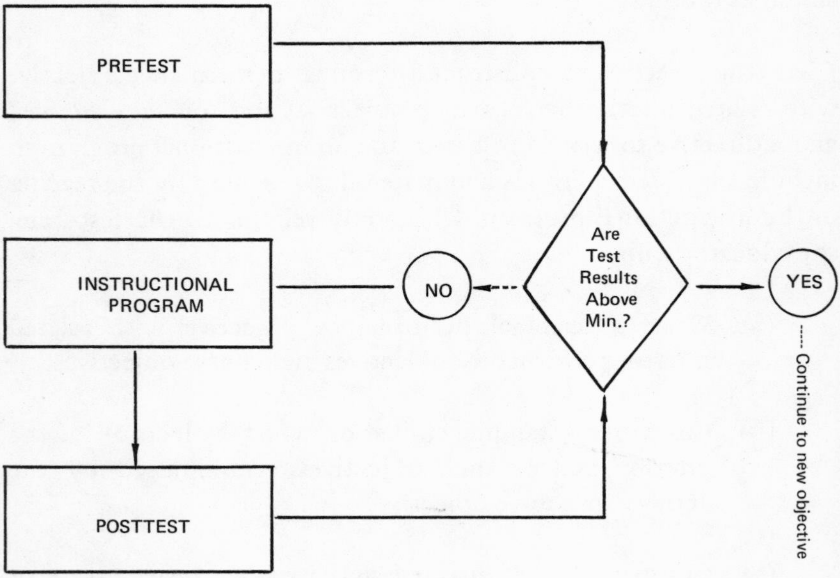

A performance objective is constructed on the accepted principle that all instruction must be operationalized in terms of student behavior. Realizing that education generally has used instructional objectives void of evaluative criteria, the need for performance objectives which clearly describe the learner's behavior at the conclusion of a sequenced instructional program becomes the rule rather than the exception.

Educators using performance objectives have an obvious advantage in developing learning sequences designed to accomplish a specific behavioral change. The specificity required of the performance objective allows for an accurate assessment of student achievement. For example, educators can effectively draw conclusions about the need to change the instructional program(s) based on the change created by the program in learner behavior(s).

Two basic evaluative tools used for assessing student achievement are:

Pretest: An assessment of a learner's skills upon entering a learning experience. The data collected on the pretest become the basis for prescribing an instructional program for the learner.

Posttest: An assessment of student skills upon completion of a prescribed instructional program. This form of evaluation measures the learner's achievement between his entry into the learning experience and his exit as described by the performance objective.

All performance objectives, whether they are terminal, interim, or course objectives, are the test items for assessing student achievement. Each describes:

The Task:	That which the learner is to do,
The Conditions:	The specifications by which the task is to be performed, and
The Criteria:	The predetermined minimum level at which the learner must perform to be considered successful.

PERFORMANCE OBJECTIVE

(Task/Conditions/Criteria)

A test item requires the learner to perform to criteria under a set of conditions as described in the performance objective. The learner is considered successful only when he can perform the established minimum criteria under those conditions at or higher than the minimum level as defined by the criteria stated in the performance objective.

The instructional program is designed to provide opportunities to develop the skills and concepts necessary to perform the tasks described in the performance objective. Other emphasis is placed on the learner's prerequisite skills upon entering the learning experience. Assessment of the learner's ability to perform both prerequisite and requisite skills is made through a pretest. The instructional program is assigned to each individual student on the basis of his performance on the pretest.

CASE PROBLEM 1

You are a mathematics teacher and have been given the following performance objective.

> Given five problem situations, necessary equipment, and a description of desired quantities of liquid which require the use of each of the following units: cup, pint, quart, gallon, at his level of instruction,* the learner will demonstrate procedures for finding the solution set as it relates to the unit of measure, with 75 percent accuracy or greater.

Read the two test items given below and select the item(s) appropriate for evaluating student performance.

(1) John needs two gallons of water. He has a five gallon pail and a three gallon pail. How can John measure two gallons of water using the given pails? Write your answer on a separate sheet. Show all your work.

(2) Given the directive to draw diagrams which illustrate the measure of one gallon of liquid using the following units: cup, pint, quart, the learner will demonstrate procedures for drawing diagrams under the following conditions:

   (a) Select one unit of measure and diagram the use of that unit to measure one gallon.
   (b) Select a combination of two units of measure and diagram the use of the units to measure one gallon.
   (c) Select a combination of three units of measure and diagram the use of the units to measure one gallon.

*Level of instruction reflects the skill and competencies of each individual learner. Materials and tasks should be developed in relationship to these indicated proficiencies.

You should have selected both of the test items listed on Page 4 as a measure of student performance. Each test item listed measures the student's performance although each test item uses a different method as a testing procedure.

Four basic methods may be used in the construction of test items. The responsibility of the educator is to consider as many different forms of test items as possible. Brief descriptions of these forms are as follows:

Constructions: A test of this type emphasizes skills which involve the learner in making or forming an item by combining parts, e.g., to draw a geometric figure within defined specifications and conditions.

Demonstrations: This type of test item requires the learner to perform by illustrating or explaining.

Observations: A test item by observation requires the learner to demonstrate procedures necessary for gathering scientific information by noting facts and then responding to the observations in a cognitive way, such as by writing his observations on paper or giving an oral report.

Paper and Pencil: Subjective and/or objective test items designed for the learner to demonstrate his proficiencies in a written form.

Action verbs and action verb phrases are used to describe that which the learner will be doing when he performs the task. The chart on the next page suggests how the learner might respond to specific tasks as described through the action verbs.

Action Verb or Action Verb Phrase	*Definition*	*Method*	*Task Examples*
Identify	Point to, touch, or pick up.	Point to, touch, pick up	—a specified object
Name	Supply a name (orally, writing, or demonstrating) for a class of objects, events, or movements.	Writing	—words or symbols
		Formulating sounds	—speaking, reading, performing on instrument or singing
		Physical movements	—gesturing, body position, and/or movement and drawing.
Describe	Naming all the necessary categories of an object, object properties, or event properties that are relevant to the description of a designated situation.	Writing	—an explanation by use of words, phrases, sentences
		Formulating sounds	—giving oral details, illustrative sound of
		Drawing	—illustrating by a series of lines or shapes of
		Physical movements	—demonstrating motion or position of
			CHARACTERISTICS OF IDEAS, EVENTS, OR OBJECTS NAMED IN OBJECTIVE
Describe Similarities and Differences	Naming categories of objects, object properties, or event properties that are potentially confusing; likewise, if two constrasting identifications	Same as *Describe* except that two or more characteristics of ideas, objects, or events named in objective are compared.	

Action Verb or Action Verb Phrase	*Definition*	*Method*	*Task Examples*
Describe Relationships	Naming categories of objects, object properties, or event properties that are comparable and related.	Same as *Describe*	except that two or more characteristics of ideas, concepts, or events named in objective are related.
State a Rule	Make a statement (orally or in written form, and not necessarily in technical terms) which conveys a rule or a principle, including the naming of proper classes of objects or events in their correct order.	Writing Speaking	—stating a rule —giving a formula, principle, and/or procedure
Demonstrate Procedures to Classify	Apply rules as stated in "State a Rule."	Writing	—words, symbols, solutions to math problems
		Formulating sounds	—giving a speech, singing, or playing an instrument
		Physical movement	—dancing, swimming, or sculpturing, drawing
Order Procedures	State rules for constructing an original experiment.	Writing	—of data according to original criteria such as large to small, least important to most important, etc.
		Formulating sounds	—of instrument or vocal scales
		Physical movements	—sequencing series of movements

(over)

Action Verb or Action Verb Phrase	*Definition*	*Method*	*Task Examples*
Demonstrate procedures to construct an experiment and/or model.	Performing operations necessary to apply rules given in "Order Procedures."	Writing	—a composition of sentences, paragraphs, and themes
		Formulating sounds	—an original instrumental arrangement
		Drawing	—an original blueprint
		Physical movement	—creative dance

CASE PROBLEM 2

Your task is to analyze the following objective.

> Given six pictures, each depicting one of the following physical characteristics of a bird: head, leg, tail, and wing, and an illustration of only the outline of the body, at his level of instruction, the learner will demonstrate procedures to classify each of the physical characteristics as each relates to its position in the structure of a bird.

Read the criteria listed below and select the item(s) which are consistent with the performance objective.

(1) A percentage deducted from a total score for each physical characteristic misplaced.

(2) Pre-established percentage deducted for each of the characteristics incorrectly placed according to a weighted scale, i.e., five points for misplaced wings, two points for misplaced tails, etc.

(3) Credit given for successful completion of the task if learner places the characteristics in the correct location on the illustration provided of the body of a bird.

You should have selected Item 3 as the only item consistent with the performance objective. The learner's performance is judged only on the basis of the criteria stated in the performance objective.

The criteria of the performance objective define the performance of the task in terms of degree of accuracy, the amount of time, or the quantity to be produced by the learner. All criteria for evaluating the task must be observable and/or measurable. The evaluator measures either the actual performance of the task (i.e., technique) or the results of the performance.

Characteristics such as creativity must be stated in specific criteria on which a theme, musical composition, etc., may be evaluated. The quality to be included in the evaluation of the given task may be too extensive to be stated in each individual performance objective. Therefore, the performance objective must name a specific reference source from which the criteria for evaluating performance may be obtained.

CASE PROBLEM 3

One of your objectives requires the student to research a topic using library references. Some of the students do not have the necessary skills to perform the task.

In analyzing the situation for a possible solution, which of the following procedures would be most appropriate in rectifying this situation?

(1) Inform students of their lack of necessary skills to function with a research topic in the library.

(2) Instruct a total group in the basic research skills.

(3) Ask the librarian to give extra help to students who lack skills.

(4) Teach research skills to all students whom the librarian indicated lacked skill to perform assigned task.

(5) Pretest all students and prepare an individualized instructional program for each on the basis of test results.

If you selected "pretest," choice No. 5, as the strategy for assessing student performance in using the library, you have selected the soundest procedure to establish a meaningful learning environment for each student.

Learners bring many experiences and much knowledge with them to a learning experience. Therefore, to capitalize on previous experiences and to make the new learning experience relevant to the learner's needs, a pretest developed from the contents of the course objective is administered. The test items on the pretest must reflect the skills and content prerequisite as well as requisite to the course objective so that an accurate analysis may be made of the skills the learner brings into the learning experience. In this way, instructional activities may be selected on an individual basis to develop student proficiencies in areas analyzed as below the minimum prescribed by the performance objective. A student may pretest out of a course objective by demonstrating proficiencies as described by the performance objective.

CASE PROBLEM 4

You are a Humanities teacher in the process of preparing an individualized program for your students. Read carefully one of your performance objectives, which is given below.

> Given descriptive data of a local surburban community which includes a description of two or more resources, a culture native to the area, and a problematic situation involving two groups (i.e., minority, ethnic) impinging upon the given geographic region each in search of a different resource, and directive to prepare a written or oral presentation at his level of instruction, the learner will demonstrate procedures for constructing a hypothesis based on the cause-effect relationship between the resources, two groups, and to include three of the following outcomes:
>
> (1) possible conflict
> (2) possible inter/intra-dependence
> (3) justification of the resources
> (4) possible changes resulting from utilization of the resources
>
> with 70 percent accuracy or greater as established by the local humanities department.

Select from the list below the activities which would be most appropriate to fulfill the objective.

(1) Listen to a resource person who is knowledgeable about the ethnic background of the residents of the community.

(2) Watch the movie, "Youth Rebel."

(3) Construct a resource map of the community emphasizing those aspects which attract groups other than the original ethnic group.

(4) Conduct a survey of the feelings of the student body and adults concerning a hypothetical change in the local community involving the influx of a minority group.

(5) Read an article about man's attempts to conserve natural resources.

You should have selected Activities 1, 3, and 4 as most appropriate to build and fortify the knowledge relative to the structure of the local community and the effects of the problematic changes. Although Activities 2 and 5 are somewhat related to the objective, neither would directly reinforce that concept emphasized in the performance objective.

All activities within the instructional program should be directly related to the performance objective. That is, all activities should either build or fortify the knowledge and/or skill emphasized by the objective.

CASE PROBLEM 5

You are a member of a team of teachers currently deciding upon the appropriate approach relative to a given objective.

> Given the definition of appropriate scientific principles, access to necessary materials, and directive to construct an operational model, at his level of instruction, the learner will build a model which demonstrates all phases of the scientific principles involved in osmosis with 75 percent accuracy or greater.

Select the activity from the list below which is most appropriate for the stated objective.

(1) A lecture to the class on the appropriate scientific principles.

(2) A seminar based on student research of the topic.

(3) Individual student research culminated by the construction of an operational model.

(4) None of the above.

You should have selected No. 3 as the most appropriate activity. This approach will offer an opportunity to capitalize on individual interest, motivation, and aptitude of the learner. The number of activities which can be developed to reflect the skills and the concepts stated in the performance objective is limited only by the skills of the educator and the characteristics of the task. Instructional activities may also be developed by the students in cooperation with the designer, using the instructional sequence of the taxonomy as the guidelines for their development.

The task described in the performance objective may reflect any level of the cognitive process. Students of all ages and aptitudes may perform at each of the cognitive levels of the taxonomy if the educator considers the entry skills of the learner and the skills required of the learner when selecting the instructional materials and methods to be used in developing the requisite skills.

CASE PROBLEM 6

Students in a tenth grade American Literature class have been assessed as having reading skills at the sixth, eighth, and twelfth grade levels. Which of the following approaches would you select as being most appropriate in the construction of an instructional program for these students?

(1) Write a set of performance objectives for each reading level, each set of objectives requiring different types of tasks.

(2) Use the same performance objectives for all three reading levels but vary the instructional materials.

(3) Use the same performance objective but evaluate the student's performance on three different criteria scales.

(4) None of the above.

Approach No. 2 is the most appropriate to the curricular design. The level of instruction of the performance task is easily adjusted by the selection of performance materials and the method of presentation. Instructional materials (printed, audio, visual, and kinesthetic) should be selected to correspond to a variety of difficulty levels.

Not only can the level of instruction be adjusted to individual differences, but the task can be developed to accommodate individual interests and perceptions.

Another meaningful way to vary the instructional level of the task is to give the students the opportunity to conduct individual research and experimentation. For example, a student might wish to study the effects of a contemporary problem by choosing to look at the changes in his church through research while others may complete the assignment through the study of music and/or art which depicts similar changes. Both studies would follow the instructional sequence of the design established by the taxonomy.

CASE PROBLEM 7

You have been assigned to teach a general math class in which a majority of the students have little interest or achievement in math skills. They have not been given opportunities to see the relationship between math and its application to their lives. As a teacher determined to "do something" with these students, which of the following instructional programs would you suggest for these students?

(1) Textbook drills in the four basic operations (addition, subtraction, multiplication, and division of whole numbers and fractions) preceded by a teacher demonstration-lecture program.

(2) An application approach in which each student may select, on the basis of interest, problems from the areas of home economics, business education, or industrial arts. The application of math skills would be preceded by a teacher demonstration-lecture of the basic operations appropriate to the application problems.

(3) None of the above.

If you selected No. 2, the application approach, you selected the program which offers the students an opportunity to see the relationship between mathematics and their interests. This program could help to motivate the students into acquiring the basic skills in mathematics.

Any instructional program should be designed to offer the learner opportunities to see the relationships between himself and his environment. The performance tasks should involve the learner in activities and offer him choices which are of interest to him as well as a source of information. Therefore, the educator in each discipline should have the ability not only to analyze a performance task but also to show creative ways in which the learner can actually interact with the contents of the discipline and his interests.

CASE PROBLEM 8

Your task is to design the first activity in an instructional sequence for the following objective. The pretest results indicate that the students do not have any of the requisite skills for the task.

> Given media and access to research materials which reflect a contemporary social issue and the directive to develop a topic in a 1200-word theme, the learner will demonstrate procedures to construct a hypothesis which:
>
> (1) describes the effects of at least two positive or negative aspects of the topic and will support each with a minimum of two statements from the research materials or media.
>
> (2) will construct his 1200-word theme based on the criteria as established by the local humanities department for the use of the rules for composition and grammar at 85 percent accuracy or greater.

Which of the tasks listed below would you select as being the first task(s) to be completed in relationship to the objective?

(1) Given a brief description of a social issue and directive to state a positive hypothesis, the learner will demonstrate procedures to state the hypothesis as it relates to the positive aspects of the topic, with 100 percent accuracy.

(2) Given a magazine article which reflects a contemporary social issue, at his level of instruction, the learner will name the social issue and the controversial aspects of the issue with 100 percent accuracy.

(3) Given a magazine article which reflects a contemporary social issue, at his level of instruction, the learner will describe the relationship between the social issue and selected statements from the media with 100 percent accuracy.

(4) None of the above.

The activity which you should have selected as the first activity in the instructional sequence is No. 2. Activities 1 and 3 are appropriate activities for the objective, but they are advanced steps in the instructional sequence. The following should clarify this point.

Activities are developed through an instructional sequence which allows the learner the opportunity to develop and fortify skills and/or knowledge which are defined by a performance objective. The development of a skill or knowledge must take place in phases or logical steps if the learner is to be successful with the learning experience. Therefore, all activities must be designed to correspond with the pattern of interim performance objectives.

An activity may be developed to fulfill the specifications of one performance objective or a series of performance objectives. In either case, the activity must reflect the specifications of each of the interim performance objectives encompassed by the activity and must be arranged in the same order as the sequence of the performance objectives. For example, if the activity is designed for a course objective written at the interpretation level, provision must be made to allow the learner to:

(a) identify the components and/or
(b) name the components
(c) describe the components and/or
(d) describe similarities and differences between two or more components
(e) describe the relationship between two or more components.

CASE PROBLEM 9

A teacher of a foreign language has available for instructional purposes a series of tapes for the given language. However, after using the tapes for three days, the teacher finds that the following conditions exist:

(a) Some of the students pretend to listen to the tapes but are actually playing with the controls of the recorder.

(b) Some of the students complain that the tape gives them headaches.

(c) The majority benefit from the instructional tapes and prove that the tapes are effective instructional media.

From the list below select the most effective method of instruction that will meet the needs, interest, and maturity of both the teacher and students.

(1) Discipline the students who misuse the tape, send complaining students to the school nurse to have their hearing checked, and continue to require all students to listen to the tapes because they are effective as an instuctional method.

(2) Give individual instruction by
  (a) allowing one group to use the tapes,
  (b) giving teacher-led instruction to the problem group until they gain a mature attitude toward taped instruction, and
  (c) giving teacher-led instruction to the group with the listening problem.

(3) None of the above.

Method 2 should have been selected as the most effective method for the given problem. Individualized instruction requires that a variety of methods be developed which meet the needs, maturity, and interest of the learner and the individual talents of the teacher. The educator should remember that no one method should be exclusively utilized. Some learning tasks lend themselves better to a specific method of instruction while others need a variety of approaches. The responsibility of the educator is to select methods that best fit the task and the learner.

The educator, when developing the method of instruction, should remember that he merely makes suggestions. This allows students some latitude to select the most effective method(s) for learning. The two basic types of instruction are group instruction and individual instruction.

Group instruction involves interacting with peers and/or adults through lectures, discussions, or seminars. Independent instruction involves viewing, reading, and/or listening to information while working independently of peers and/or adults in a learning situation.

CASE PROBLEM 10

A student indicates that he has completed all of the activities required of him in the instructional sequence as designed in the following objective:

> Given an instrument and measures of rhythmic notation to include notes, rests, bar lines, staff, and clefs, at his level of instruction, the learner will describe, by playing on his instrument, the relationship between the given measures of music and the notation with 100 percent accuracy.

From the following list of test procedures, select the most appropriate test item to evaluate the student's performance.

(1) Pencil and paper essay test.

(2) Playing appropriate measures of music on his instrument.

(3) Oral description of the function of notations (notes, rests, bar lines, staff, and clefs).

(4) All of the above.

(5) None of the above.

Test item No. 2 is the most appropriate test item to evaluate the student's performance using the music objective. The objective requires that the learner describe the relationship between notations printed in the music and rhythm by playing his instrument.

This test item and the evaluation of the test must be identical to the task, conditions, and criteria described by the performance objective. A student who can demonstrate proficiency as described by a performance objective should be allowed to continue in the instructional sequence by advancing to the next performance objective. A student who does not demonstrate the required proficiencies is recycled into an instructional program for purposes of correcting his deficiencies.

CASE PROBLEM 11

A performance objective states that the learner is to write a composition in which he discusses social reforms in the United States. Some of the students in your class were unable to perform on the posttest with the minimum degree of accuracy because they were unable to draw the necessary relationships between social issues and social reform.

Read carefully the following suggested solutions to the problem. Select from the list the solution you think most appropriate.

(1) Pass the students on to the next objective even though they were below the minimum as stated in the performance objective as you think the concept will become clearer in the next objective.

(2) Recycle the students to the portion of the objective that they have not successfully completed until they can perform with the minimum degree of accuracy.

(3) Pass the students on to the next objective on a "condition"—if they pass the posttest on the next objective, they will be given credit for this objective.

(4) None of the above.

Solution No. 2 should have been selected as the best solution to the problem. A post-assessment of a performance objective should reflect the proficiencies and/or deficiencies of the learner. A well-stated performance objective gives a minimum level of acceptable behavior, which gives the teacher the criteria on which to determine whether the learner should be permitted to proceed in the instructional sequence or whether he should be recycled into additional practice activities allowing him to gain necessary proficiencies to continue in the instructional sequence.

The appropriate sequence in designing instructional materials and its application to practical situations have been presented through the use of case problems with an accompanying explanation for each. This presentation of practical situations should have given you, the educator, the skills necessary to design and select materials, suggest methods, and construct test items that reflect the stated performance objectives.

A series of questions to be presented on the following pages serve as a test of your skills. Read each question carefully and respond to each by placing a checkmark opposite each correct answer. (Some questions may have more than one correct answer.) To be considered successful, you must perform with 100 percent accuracy. Therefore, WORK CAREFULLY!

(1) A cycle for presenting an instructional program:

.....a. Pretest, Instructional Program, Posttest
.....b. Pretest, Posttest
.....c. Instructional Program, Posttest
.....d. Pretest, Instructional Program, Posttest, Instructional Program, Posttest
.....e. Pretest

(2) The functions of a pretest are:

.....a. to assess learner's ability to perform requisite skills and knowledge
.....b. to assess learner's ability to perform prerequisite skills.
.....c. to assign an instructional program.
.....d. all of the above
.....e. none of the above

(3) Any instructional program should include activities for:

.....a. building prerequisite skills as well as requisite skills and knowledge
.....b. building only knowledge of content at his level of instruction
.....c. enabling learner to acquire knowledge of content based on individual aptitudes for the inquiry and communication skills
.....d. building inquiry and communication skills through use of content
.....e. building inquiry and communication skills without the use of content

(4) The criteria for developing a test item to assess student achievement are:

.....a. only specified by the action
.....b. only specified by the task
.....c. only specified by the conditions
.....d. a combination of the task, action verb, and conditions.
.....e. none of the above

(5) If any learner achieves below the minimum on a given posttest, the learner will:

.....a. continue to new objective
.....b. recycle through previously completed instructional program using same content
.....c. recycle through previously completed instructional program or parts thereof using different content
.....d. continue on to new objective while being tutored on the old
.....e. retake posttest immediately using a different form

Correct your answers on Page 30 with the answers provided below:

1. a, d
2. d
3. a, c, d
4. d
5. c

If you were 100 percent correct, continue with the posttest given on Page 36. If you answered any one question incorrectly, continue on Page 32.

The cycle for the presentation of an instruction program normally follows the pattern of Pretest, Instructional Program, and Posttest.

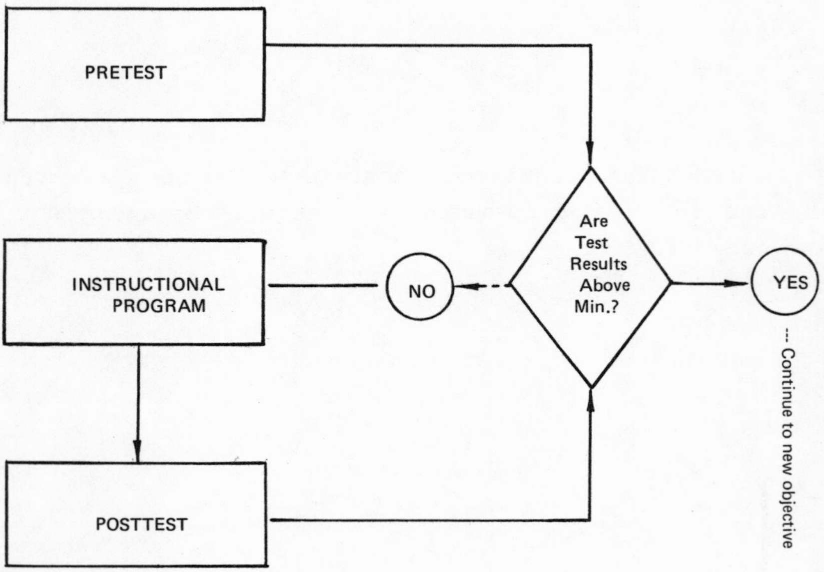

However, note the diamond-shaped form which says: "Are test results above minimum?" At this point in the cycle a decision is made as to whether the student enters the same instructional program or whether he is allowed to move on to the next objective. The decision is made on the results of the pretest. If the student is able to perform both prerequisite and requisite skills required by the objective, he may be allowed to continue to the next objective. If, however, the pretest points up a deficiency in either requisite or prerequisite skills, the learner will be assigned an appropriate instructional program to build on these deficiencies.

The function of an instructional program is to build on both prerequisite and requisite skills using content. In order to achieve the system objectives (inquiry and communication) the activities will, of course, emphasize these skills. These skills should be emphasized by all subject areas, while realizing that they cannot be developed in and of themselves but need content to help fortify them. Furthermore, all content presented to the learner must be presented at his level of instruction as determined by his present inquiry and communication skills.

Upon completion of an instructional program, the learner is again subjected to a test—this time a posttest. The function of this evaluation is to determine whether the learner can perform at the minimum level of proficiency described by the performance objective. If he can, he is promoted to the next objective. If his proficiency is below the minimum, the learner is recycled back into an instructional program to improve on those deficiencies. His new program will generally have different learning activities than the original program. The learner is again posttested. Upon passing the posttest, he then continues to the subsequent objective.

Continue with a remedial test item given on Page 34.

CASE PROBLEM 12 (Remedial Test Item)

An essay item was given to a group of students to satisfy the following objective:

> Given a problematic situation involving the conservation of one resource in a given geographic region and directive to write a 1500-word essay with footnotes and bibliography, at his level of instruction, the learner will demonstrate procedures to construct a prediction indicating the trends of the next decade by using a minimum of four references, each showing the utilization of the resources during the past decade, with 70 percent accuracy or greater as specified for essays by Warriner's English handbook.

In assessing the essays of the students, the teacher found that the students had the skills to perform the required research but were unable to demonstrate the minimum writing proficiencies as specified in Warriner's English handbook. Your critique of the case problem would recommend:

(a) A revision of the writing criteria.

(b) An alteration of the posttesting procedures to include other types of tests.

(c) A pretest of both research and writing skills, the results of which should be used in preparing the instructional program for each student.

(d) Recycling of students into an instructional program to improve writing skills.

(e) Passing students on to the next objective because they exhibited minimum performance on research skills but emphasizing writing skills on the subsequent objective.

The answers you should have selected for Case Problem 12 are "c" and "d." If you answered correctly, continue on Page 36. If you were incorrect, ask for additional help concerning the instructional cycle.

(6) The action verb "name" when used in a performance objective can be measured by which of the following types of tests:

.....a. construction-type test
.....b. demonstration-type test
.....c. observation-type test
.....d. essay-type test
.....e. all of the above
.....f. none of the above

(7) The action verb "demonstrate procedures to classify" when used in a performance objective can be measured by which of the following types of tests:

.....a. construction-type test
.....b. demonstration-type test
.....c. observation-type test
.....d. essay-type test
.....e. all of the above
.....f. none of the above

(8) The action verb "order procedures" when used in a performance objective can be measured by which of the following types of tests:

.....a. construction-type test
.....b. demonstration-type test
.....c. observation-type test
.....d. essay-type test
.....e. all of the above
.....f. none of the above

(9) Criteria for evaluating any task must be:

.....a. both observable and measurable
.....b. described by the performance objective
.....c. both of the above
.....d. none of the above

(10) Specific criteria may be stated in terms of·

.....a. amount of time
.....b. quantity to be produced
.....c. degree of accuracy
.....d. all of the above
.....e. none of the above

Compare your answers on Page 36 with the answers provided below:

6. e
7. e
8. e
9. a
10. d

If you answered all questions correctly, continue on Page 42. If you were incorrect in any of your answers, continue on Page 38.

There are four types of test forms which may be constructed for measurement of student performance: Construction, Demonstration, Observation, and/or Paper and Pencil (see Page 5 for complete description of each form). Although the type of task or the conditions under which the task must be performed may dictate the components for a test, no one specific form is required.

The criterion used to evaluate student performance must be both *Observable* and *Measurable*. Exact criterial specifications may be described in the performance objective in terms of *amount of time, quantity to be produced, degree of accuracy,* or *any combination of the three.*

Continue with a remedial test item given on Page 39.

.ASE PROBLEM 13 (Remedial Test Item)

The following performance objective has been written for a general math class:

> Given necessary equipment and the measure of two of the three angles in a triangle, at his level of instruction, the learner will demonstrate procedures for obtaining the measurement of the third angle with accuracy within 2 degrees or less.

Three separate test forms were prepared to evaluate student performance on this objective. These forms are as follows:

(1) Given a protractor and the degrees of two of the three angles of a triangle, the learner will construct a triangle from the given angles and name the measurement of the third angle within 2 degrees' accuracy or greater.

(2) Given a construction of a triangle, the measurement of two of the three angles, and a protractor, at his level of instruction, the learner will demonstrate procedures to find the measurement of the third angle with the protractor within 2 degrees' accuracy or greater.

(3) Given the measurement of two angles of a triangle and directive to find the measurement of the third angle through use of a formula, at his level of instruction, the learner will demonstrate procedures to find the solution set of the third angle within 2 degrees' accuracy or greater.

Your critique of the case problem as given would describe:

(a) An inconsistency between the task on Posttest Item No. 3 and the task described by the performance objective.

(b) An inconsistency between the conditions on Posttest Item No. 2 and the conditions described by the performance objective.

CASE PROBLEM 13 (Continued)

(c) Limitation of each of the posttest evaluations to a construction-type test.

(d) Limitation of each of the posttest evaluations to a demonstration-type test.

(e) No inconsistencies between any of the posttest items and the performance objective.

You should have selected "e" as the correct answer for Case Problem 13. If you answered correctly, continue on Page 42. If you were incorrect in your selection, ask for additional help concerning type of evaluation.

(11) Evaluative criteria for assessing student achievement are described by:

.....a. the pretest

.....b. the posttest

.....c. the performance objective

.....d. a standardized scale

.....e. a curriculum guide for each course

(12) Activities in any instructional program should be developed on the basis of:

.....a. learner's aptitude, interest, and maturity as well as skills and knowledge described by the performance objective

.....b. skills described by the performance objective

.....c. interest, aptitude, and maturity of learner

.....d. the content covered by the activities

.....e. the content of the subject and the maturity level of the learner

(13) The learner's interest can be developed in an instructional program by:

.....a. offering opportunities for the learner to see the relationships between himself and his environment

.....b. allowing opportunities for learner to interact with content

.....c. allowing opportunities for learner to further develop his interests

.....d. allowing opportunities for learner to make choices

Compare your answers given on Page 42 with the correct answers provided below:

11. c
12. a
13. a, b, c, d

If you answered all questions correctly, continue on Page 47. If, however, you were incorrect in any of your answers, continue on Page 44.

How a learner is to demonstrate his achievement at the end of the instructional program is explicitly described by the performance objective. The criteria described by the performance objective become the basis for evaluating performance on both the pretest and the posttests.

The criteria of the performance objective serve as a guide to the teacher in helping the learner to identify or develop his proficiencies. What the learner does to develop the proficiencies described by the criteria is only guided somewhat by the performance objective. The description of the task and the conditions under which the task is to be performed describe the skills required of the learner. How these skills are developed is limited, then, only by the imagination and creativity of the educator. In the development of the activities, the educator should give careful consideration to the interest, aptitude, and maturity of the learner.

The effectiveness of the activities is enhanced by opportunities for the learner to relate the subject to himself and his environment.

Complete the remedial test item given on Page 45.

CASE PROBLEM 14

An objective for a speech course is as follows:

> Given directive to prepare and deliver a ten-minute demonstration and 48 hours of preparation time, at his level of instruction, the learner will demonstrate procedures to select a topic, organize a demonstration, construct props, and deliver the speech with 75 percent accuracy or greater as determined by the rating on the local school district Evaluation Criteria Form.

Your critique of this objective would recommend:

(a) The deletion of the requirement to "select a topic" and the addition of "given a specific topic" because a given topic would "truly test the learner's speaking ability."

(b) The retention of "select a topic," as this aspect of the performance objective could have the capacity to add interest and motivation for the learner.

You should have selected "b" as the correct answer to Case Problem 14. If you answered correctly, continue on Page 47. If you were incorrect, ask for additional instruction concerning development of student activities.

(14) Which procedure(s) is used to develop student skill and knowledge of proficiency?:

.....a. performance objectives
.....b. pretests
.....c. instructional program—methods and materials
.....d. all of the above
.....e. none of the above

(15) To provide the learner with the appropriate instructional sequence, any activity should be patterned after:

.....a. a series of course objectives
.....b. a series of terminal performance objectives
.....c. a series of discipline objectives.
.....d. a series of interim performance objectives
.....e. none of the above.

(16) A measurable change in learner behavior is evaluated by:

.....a. measuring actual performance against predetermined and specific criteria
.....b. measuring the results of performance against predetermined and specific criteria
.....c. both of the above
.....d. neither of the above

Compare your answers on Page 47 with the correct answers provided below:

14. c
15. d
16. c

If you answered all questions correctly, continue on Page 52. If you were incorrect in answering any question, continue on Page 49.

Skills and knowledge described by a performance objective are developed through assignment of the learner to an appropriate instructional program consisting of individually selected materials and a variety of methods.

All activities in the instructional sequence should be developed to the performance objectives to include the course objective or terminal performance when appropriate. This sequence will allow the learner to systematically acquire the skills and knowledge necessary to perform the terminal performance objective.

Whether or not the learner has acquired the skills and knowledge described by the objective can be determined by administering a test to evaluate his performance or the results of his performance. Activities are an indication of the learner's progress toward terminal behavior but activities are not to be used as an evaluation of his behavior.

Complete the remedial test item provided on Page 50.

CASE PROBLEM 15 (Remedial Test Item)

The overcrowded conditions of the library make it necessary for each teacher using the library to aid the librarians in locating references for the students. Therefore, in fulfilling the research activities for the following objective, the classroom teacher brought the necessary books to the classroom for each individual student.

> Given a problematic situation involving the utilization of one resource in a given geographic region and a directive to write a 1500-word essay with footnotes and bibliography, at his level of instruction, the learner will demonstrate procedures to construct a prediction indicating the trends of the next decade by using a minimum of four references, each showing the utilization of the resources during the past decade, with 70 percent accuracy or greater as specified for essays by the local humanities department.

The posttest in which the learner fulfills the requirements for the objective requires him to locate and research references in the library. Your critique of the case problem would recommend:

(a) the task required in the posttest be consistent with the task required in the activities leading to the posttest.

(b) the activity as described by the performance objective be more realistic under the imposed limitations.

(c) the alteration of the performance objective to include "given appropriate references."

You should have selected "b" as the correct answer to Case Problem 15. If you answered correctly, continue on Page 52. If you were incorrect in your answer, discuss this aspect of constructing activities with your instructor or a colleague.

(17) Specifications describing how the task is to be performed are known as ....

(18) The contents of any pretest must include:

.....a. contents of course objective only
.....b. inquiry and communication skills emphasized in objective.
.....c. prerequisite skills
.....d. requisite skills and contents of course objective
.....e. requisite skills only

(19) If pretest results are minimum or greater, the learner may:
.....a. continue to new objective
.....b. follow a modified instructional program.
.....c. follow an instructional program but at a more difficult level than the other students
.....d. do work for extra credit
.....e. posttest

Compare your answers on Page 52 with the correct answers provided below:

17. conditions
18. b, c, d
19. a

If you answered all questions correctly, continue on Page 57. If you were incorrect in any of your answers, continue on Page 54.

The conditions stated in the performance objective describe how the learner must perform the task. The educator must analyze each performance objective for both requisite and prerequisite skills required of the learner. Therefore, the function of the pretest is to determine which skills and knowledge the learner now possesses, and on the basis of this information he can be assigned to the appropriate activities. If, for example, the learner possesses all prerequisite and requisite skills and knowledges, he may continue to the new objective in the course.

Complete the remedial posttest item given on Page 55.

CASE PROBLEM 16 (Remedial Test Item)

Given the dimensions of five rectangles, at his level of instruction the learner will demonstrate procedures to correctly calculate the area of four of the five rectangles.

The following pretest was prepared to evaluate skills and knowledge relative to the above given objective.

Instructions: Find the area of four of the five rectangles given in the test form. Use the formula: A = L x W

Your critique of the case problem as given would describe:

(a) an inconsistency between the task on the pretest and the task described by the performance objective.

(b) an inconsistency between the conditions on the pretest and the conditions described by the performance objective.

(c) an inconsistency between the criteria on the pretest and the criteria described by the performance objective.

(d) no inconsistencies between the pretest and the performance objective.

You should have selected "b" as the correct answer to Case Problem 16. If you answered correctly, continue on Page 57. If you were incorrect, ask your instructor or a colleague for additional explanations of the relationship between a performance objective and a pretest.

(20) A performance objective describes:

.....a. the learner's minimum behavior at the conclusion of the instructional program

.....b. the learner's behavior before entering the instructional program

.....c. the minimum behavior acceptable of all learners

.....d. the amount of change desired of all learners

.....e. ideal learner behavior toward which all learners should strive

(21) An instructional program is prescribed on the basis of:

.....a. pretest results

.....b. previous posttest results

.....c. standardized testing scores

.....d. previous performance

.....e. none of the above

(22) A teacher may find information regarding the task for measuring learner performance at the end of the instructional program in:

.....a. a performance objective

.....b. an accepted reference

.....c. a reference specified by the performance objective.

.....d. the teacher's manual to the text being used

.....e. none of the above

Compare your answers on Page 57 with the answers provided below:

20. a, c
21. a, d
22. a, c

If you answered all questions correctly, continue on Page 62. If you were incorrect in any answer, continue on Page 59.

A performance objective describes how the behavior of the learner will be different at the end of the instructional program. This behavior, of course, is the minimum acceptable by all learners. Some learners may have been able to perform at the minimum level upon taking the pretest. If you will recall, these learners are allowed to continue to the next objective. Some learners, however, may have been deficient in many prerequisite as well as requisite skills. The amount of change desired of this learner is greater as compared to those who pretested out of the instructional program. The instructional program designed to obtain the desired behavior will be assigned on the basis of the pretest as well as previous performance. This is to say, that if the teacher has knowledge of the methods most effective with the learner, he will use this knowledge to prescribe appropriate methods and materials.

At the completion of the instructional program the teacher will again make reference to the performance objective for the development of a posttest to assess whether the learner has achieved the desired behaviors as described by the performance objective.

Complete the remedial test item given on Page 60.

CASE PROBLEM 17 (Remedial Test Item)

A teacher of an advanced biology class finds upon analysis of the results of a pretest of students entering his class that the students appear to have little knowledge of the characteristics of the common insect families or scientific classes of insects. He discovers upon further investigation that the teacher of basic biology begins a unit in the study of insects each year by taking the students to the open fields with a directive to catch as many insects as possible for a collection. Upon returning to the classroom, the teacher then supplies the students with a key containing appropriate information to allow the students to classify insects by family names and scientific classes to fulfill the objective given below:

> Given a specimen from each of ten common insect families and five scientific classes, at his level of instruction, the learner will name by family name and scientific class each specimen collected to include specimens from five classes and ten families named with 90 percent accuracy or greater.

Your critique of the case problems would recommend:

(a) The teacher of advanced biology to teach the characteristics of the insect families and scientific class if that skill is prerequisite to advanced biology objectives.

(b) The terminal performance objective for basic biology should be altered to require the learner to pass an objective-type test on the characteristics of insects before he is given credit for the course objective on insects.

(c) The revision of the course objective for basic biology to include a series of interim performance objectives which would allow the learner to identify, name, describe, describe similarities and differences, and describe relationship between given insect families and their characteristics.

(d) All of the above.

You should have selected "a" and "c" as the correct answers to Case Problem 17. If you answered correctly, continue on Page 62. If, however, you answered incorrectly, ask your instructor or a colleague for additional help with this phase of the program.

(23) The portion of a performance objective that is stated as the "level of instruction" refers to:

.....a. only the reading and writing skills of the learner

.....b. all inquiry and communication skills

.....c. I.Q. of the learner

.....d. all of the above

(24) Individualized instruction requires that a variety of methods be used to develop individual needs, maturity, and interest of the learner. Which of the following instructional methods are excluded from use in an individual program?

.....a. independent study

.....b. lecture

.....c. seminar

.....d. all of the above

.....e. none of the above

Compare your answers on Page 62 with the correct answers provided below:

23. b
24. e

If you answered both questions correctly, continue on Page 67. If you answered either of the questions incorrectly, continue on Page 64.

Learners entering a classroom are individuals, each with special learning capabilities and problems. An instructional program cannot, of course, allow for all individual differences, but it can be constructed to compensate for some of the very common instructional differences. Therefore, the term "level of instruction" refers to individual student differences as measured by the inquiry and communication skills and should be criteria for selecting the methods and materials for individual students.

Individualized instruction does not necessarily exclude any method which involves the learner with small or large groups of students. Individualized instruction excludes only those methods which are deemed ineffective as means by which a learner can learn. The instructional environment must include activities which allow students to interact with one another, but the instructional program must be designed to allow for rate of achievement and interest of each student. Some learners must be involved with their peers in the instructional program while the rate of achievement and interests of other learners merit activities involving only the individual.

Complete the remedial test item provided on Page 65.

CASE PROBLEM 18 (Remedial Test Item)

A teacher of psychology has designed a variety of activities to develop the skills/concepts necessary to allow a learner to perform as described by the following objective:

> Given ten case studies involving group behavior and directive to write 1000 words to explain the significance of the behavior exhibited in each of the case studies, the learner will construct an essay as the response to each case study, in which he names psychological principles and theories of group behavior present, and describes the same with examples drawn from the case study, with 75 percent accuracy or greater as established by local school district criteria for writing of research papers.

The activities which have been designed include:

(1) Individual research of group behavior in specified situations. This research may be completed by experimentation.

(2) Lecture, reading, seminars, and other small-group interaction-type activities.

(3) Case studies approach relative to specific principles and theories.

Your critique of the case problem would recommend:

(a) That only a case study approach be taken.

(b) That a variety of methods (as suggested) be used to accommodate individual interest and aptitudes.

(c) That experimentation is too complex for secondary level students.

You should have selected "b" as the correct answer to Case Problem 18. If you answered correctly, continue on Page 67. If you were incorrect, ask your instructor or a colleague for additional information relative to construction of instructional programs which compensate for individual differences.

The next phase of this program is designed to involve you in demonstrating practical application of the skills necessary in constructing an instructional program. Follow all directions given in the following pages.

Step 1: Write a Terminal Performance Objective and the accompanying Interim Performance Objectives for a unit of study in your own subject area. (For a review of writing performance objectives refer to Pages 62-71 of *How to Classify a Performance Objective.*)

Terminal
Performance
Objective ....
....
....
....
....
....

Interim
Performance
Objectives ....
....
....
....
....
....

Step 2: Construct a Course Objective for one or more of the Interim Performance Objectives constructed in Step 1. (For a review, refer to Pages 73-77 of *How to Classify a Performance Objective.*) Name IPOs included.

....

Course
Objective ....

....

....

....

....

....

Step 3: Construct a test item for the Course Objective written in Step 2. Be sure that the test item is inclusive of all the interim steps (Interim Performance Objectives) included in the Course Objective.

Step 4: Construct an activity that reflects two or more of the Interim Performance Objectives included in the Course Objective. Specify on the line provided which of the IPOs are included in the activity......................................

....

Step 5: Describe methods and materials that could be used to develop each of the Interim Performance Objectives not included in the activity. Include a description of methods and materials for at least three levels of instruction. Be specific.

CONCLUSION: UTILIZATION OF COMPONENTS FOR INDIVIDUALIZING INSTRUCTION

"Meeting the needs of individual students" is a simple phrase, but one which describes a major problem confronting every classroom teacher—a problem to which a majority of educators throughout the nation have not yet found a satisfactory solution. The objective of this volume, in combination with each of the other volumes in the series of four, is to assist the teacher and instructional designer to develop instructional programs with the capacity to capitalize on the individual strengths and potentialities of each student.

The flood of innovations in education provides opportunities for each learner to achieve optimum personal growth. However, the problem for educators is to combine in the right proportions the ideas with the available human and material resources. An instructional system as presented in this series has the capacity to maximize the possibilities to obtain the "right proportion" and consequently reach desired educational results. This is achieved by the following:

1. Planning a course of action which gives consideration to the conditions which affect and which produce the desired outcome.

2. Writing performance objectives which describe (a) conditions, (b) tasks, (c) desired outcomes, and (d) criteria for evaluating specific performance.

3. Classifying performance objectives to include (a) interpretation of the taxonomy of cognitive skills, (b) construction of a sequence of objectives: terminal performance objectives, interim performance objectives, and course objectives.

4. Developing instructional methods, materials, and instructional strategies for attaining the desired outcomes defined by the objectives.